EARTH VERSE

Haiku from the Ground Up

For Hannah Mahoney, haiku poet and copyeditor extraordinaire,
and for those who, late at night, count syllables instead of sheep
S. M. W.

For Mark Brimble — a force of nature
W. G.

First edition 2018

Library of Congress Catalog Card Number pending
ISBN 978-0-7636-7512-7

17 18 19 20 21 22 TLF 10 9 8 7 6 5 4 3 2 1

Printed in Dongguan, Guangdong, China

This book was typeset in Intro Book and Dante Regular.
The illustrations were done in colored pencil.

Candlewick Press
99 Dover Street
Somerville, Massachusetts 02144

visit us at www.candlewick.com

EARTH VERSE

Haiku from the Ground Up

SALLY M. WALKER

illustrated by **WILLIAM GRILL**

CANDLEWICK PRESS

third one from the sun,
Earth's blue and white majesty
dwarfs her lunar child

fragile outer crust,
shell around mantle and core—
Earth: a hard-boiled egg

gold, silver, copper,
sapphires, rubies, emeralds —
glittery Earth-bling

cleaved into thin sheets,
mica's panes invite sunlight —
natural window

molten magma stew
bubbles out of its hot pot,
chills into hard rock

layered sediments
stuck tight with mineral glue
build layered Earth-stripes

check out a new look:
metamorphic makeover
turns granite to gneiss

unscalable cliff —
canyon's stone-faced guardian
forever on watch

silica, ghost-like,
drifts into wood and shouts, "Boo!"—
petrified forest

nestled in sandstone,
Maiasaura shields her young
fossil family

energy unleashed
shoots waves through the brittle crust —
trees topple down cliffs

seafloor tug-of-war:
a tsunami drowns the shore,
neighborhoods vanish

hotheaded mountain
loses its cool, spews ash cloud —
igneous tantrum

pyroclastic flow
rushes down Vesuvius . . .
a ghost dog lingers

fiery fingers
painting Earth orange and black —
swirly pahoehoe

hot rock meets cold sea,
shatters lava to black sand . . .
a crab tiptoes home

sky shenanigans:
lightning bullies storm clouds with
thunderous results

birds sleep in their nests
winds unfurl a fog blanket . . .
leaves sing lullabies

mountain stream rushes,
ancient river meanders —
hare and tortoise race

a flat stone, skipping,
casts circles across the lake,
lassoing the fish

sediment-filled waves
tumble in a frothy foam . . .
a gull wears sand socks

no bucket needed,
the sea builds its own castle . . .
flowers bloom on dunes

deep layers of ice:
a continent-size blanket —
Earth's crust mattress sags

relentless glaciers
pluck and smooth steep valley walls,
changing V to U

ready for the plunge,
ice slides off rocky playgrounds
and calves with a splash

titanic iceberg
buoyantly cruises the deep —
ship, keep your distance!

underground water
trickles through a sandstone sponge,
pools inside the well

hold fast, stalactite,
everlasting icicle,
stone bed for a bat

stalagmite! reach high!
catch the ceiling's drip, drip, drip,
grow up from the ground

EARTH

In some ways, Earth is rather like a hard-boiled egg. The crust, Earth's outer layer, is a brittle shell that can easily crack and shatter under pressure. The mantle, Earth's thick middle layer, bends like the white part of the hard-boiled egg. It's made of hot, squeezable rock that oozes and flows without breaking. Earth's center, or core, is made up of two parts: a solid inner core surrounded by a liquid outer core. The temperature where the two parts touch each other is as hot as the surface of the sun.

Earth's moon was an accident, the result of a humongous crash. Scientists believe that Earth was hit by a celestial body about half its size. The fiery impact threw tons of Earth's crust and mantle into space. Earth's gravitational pull kept the mantle debris orbiting Earth like a cosmic Hula-Hoop. Over tens of thousands of years, the orbiting debris combined and formed the moon.

MINERALS

Minerals are solid, non-living substances found in nature. Each mineral has its own special arrangement of atoms. Those arrangements create many interesting shapes. Some minerals are long, pointy crystals. Others are shaped like cubes. Some look like heaps of soap bubbles. The way a mineral's atoms are arranged means that when the mineral breaks, it does so in certain ways. The mineral mica breaks apart into sheets that are almost paper-thin.

Depending on its chemical ingredients, a mineral can be any color found in the rainbow. Minerals can be hard or soft. Diamonds, rubies, and sapphires are hard enough to scratch glass. Yet people can powder their skin with talc, a mineral so soft your fingernail can scratch it. The mineral quartz is made of a chemical compound called silica. Most seashore sand grains are quartz. Silica is one of the main ingredients used to make glass.

Our homes would be stark, boring places without minerals. Paint, wallboard, floor tiles, and screws all contain minerals, as do sidewalk and road pavements. And pencils write with the mineral graphite.

ROCKS

Rocks form when minerals crystallize (solidify) or when natural processes cement pieces of minerals and broken rock together. Earth's three main groups of rock are known as igneous, sedimentary, and metamorphic.

Igneous rocks begin as magma. Born in the mantle, magma is toothpaste-thick, fiery-hot melted rock. It oozes upward into the crust or onto Earth's surface, where it cools into a solid igneous rock. Many roads are built on top of a bed of crushed basalt, an abundantly found igneous rock.

Tiny pieces of broken rock are called sediments. Broken shells and bone are sediments, too. Water, wind, and ice sweep sediments from one place to another. They deposit them in accumulating layers that can be thousands of feet thick. Sometimes the weight of the top layers squeezes the sediments in the lower layers so tightly together that they become hard rock. Other times, water containing dissolved minerals seeps into loose sediments. When the dissolved minerals crystallize, they glue the sediments together. Rock formed from hardened or cemented sediments is called sedimentary rock. Sandstone, frequently used as a building stone, is a sedimentary rock.

Heat and pressure change a rock's texture and structure. They force a rock's minerals to rearrange themselves in new patterns. Some of the minerals may chemically change into a different mineral. A rock that has been changed by heat and pressure is called a metamorphic rock. Under heat and pressure, the sedimentary rock called limestone becomes the metamorphic rock called marble. Artists sculpt statues in marble. The igneous rock called granite becomes gneiss.

FOSSILS

Giant bones or razor-sharp teeth may be all that's left of lumbering dinosaurs and sharks longer than a school bus, but their hardened remains, called fossils, can teach us a lot about ancient life-forms. But fossils are much more than just bones and teeth. Skin, eggs, nests, footprints, and even a worm's trail can be fossils. The leaves, flowers, and stems of a plant can become a fossil, too. When any of these items is naturally preserved, its fossil is like a stone photograph of ancient life-forms and the environments they lived in.

Most fossils are found in sedimentary rock. That's because the remains were buried by sediments, which protected them from destruction. The remains later hardened into rock along with the sediment. But naturally occurring chemicals dissolved in water can also seep into the pores of bones and wood. Inside the pores, the chemicals combine and form a mineral. When the mineral crystallizes, the bone or piece of wood turns into stone. The fossilized tree trunks found in Petrified Forest National Park, in Arizona, formed this way.

EARTHQUAKES

Forces inside Earth squeeze and stretch the rock that make up its brittle crust. When forces push or pull the rock too much, it cracks. But they still keep squeezing and stretching. That causes energy to build up inside the cracked rock. Sometimes the energy becomes more than the rock can bear. Suddenly, the rock on one side of the crack jerks loose from the rock on the other side. Waves of energy ripple away from the crack, now called a fault. The traveling waves make the rock vibrate and quake. Earthquakes damage buildings and roads and can cause landslides. Earthquakes beneath an ocean can trigger a water wave called a tsunami. By the time a tsunami reaches land, it can be fifty to one hundred feet tall. A tsunami's power can wipe out everything in its path.

VOLCANOES

A volcano can be a towering mountain, a small hill, an enormous crater, or a crack on the ocean floor. A volcano forms whenever magma erupts onto Earth's surface. When magma reaches the surface, it is called lava. Lava can have very different appearances. The surface of pahoehoe lava is smooth and ropy, while another kind of lava, called aa, is rough and sharp.

Volcanoes spew steamy clouds that contain fragments of magma and rock called pyroclasts. Sometimes a cloud of boiling-hot pyroclasts collapses and rushes down a volcano's flanks. Traveling at speeds up to hundreds of miles per hour, a pyroclastic flow destroys everything in its path. The pyroclastic flow that occurred after Mount Vesuvius erupted in 79 CE killed nearly 16,000 people and buried the towns of Pompeii and Herculaneum. It buried animals as well—even a dog. The pyroclasts hardened and became a stone mold around the bodies. Casts made from these molds become ghostly reminders of lost lives.

ATMOSPHERIC AND SURFACE WATER

In a never-ending pattern called the hydrologic cycle, Earth's water moves back and forth between the planet and its atmosphere. In the air, we see it as clouds, fog, rain, and snow. On Earth's surface, it becomes rivers, lakes, oceans, and deep layers of ice. Part of the hydrologic cycle lies hidden beneath our feet. Water trickles through the air spaces between grains of sediment and soil and inside the pores of sedimentary rock. It flows, hidden, deep inside cracks in Earth's bedrock, the thick layers of rock often covered by soil or large bodies of water. Also unseen, water heated by the sun evaporates and returns to the atmosphere.

Oceans hold about 97 percent of the water on Earth. Slightly more than 2 percent is frozen in huge moving bodies of ice called glaciers. About 1 percent is found flowing in rivers, inside bedrock, or in lakes. Earth's atmosphere contains only a sliver, much less than 1 percent, of our planet's water. When a lightning bolt super-heats a storm cloud (water in the atmosphere), the column of air surrounding the bolt expands and contracts. The column of air claps loudly, then vibrates in a rumble of thunder.

GLACIERS

In very cold places, some snowflakes never completely melt. Instead, they become rounded, icy grains that accumulate in layers from year to year. Up to one hundred years may pass before the weight of the layers squeezes all the air from the tiny spaces between the grains. When almost all the air is gone, the icy grains become glacial ice.

Glacial ice fills bowl-shaped hollows near mountaintops. In frigid Antarctica, miles-deep ice sheets blanket most of the continent. No matter where thick ice layers form, the upper layers press hard enough on the ice below to make the lower layers bend. The ice starts moving the way a ball of soft clay moves when it is pressed flat. And it will keep flowing, even across flat land. Once a huge mass of ice starts flowing, it is called a glacier. Gigantic glaciers are so heavy that Earth's crust sags beneath their weight.

Glaciers have tremendous power. A glacier that flows into a V-shaped mountain valley plucks rock from its walls, scouring them into a broad U-shaped valley. Glaciers often carry gigantic boulders from one place to another. When a glacier shoves into the sea, huge chunks of ice calve, or break off, from the glacier's edge and float away as icebergs. In 1912, if the *Titanic* hadn't encountered an iceberg, it probably would have arrived safely in New York City.

GROUNDWATER

Beneath Earth's surface, water travels through bedrock in the tiny air spaces between the rock's mineral and sediment grains. When people drill a well, it fills with this water, which is called groundwater.

Most caves form when groundwater trickles inside cracks found in bedrock (a thick layer of buried rock) that is made of limestone, a sedimentary rock. Acids found naturally in groundwater slowly dissolve the bedrock, enlarging the cracks and creating a large open space. A cave can be a single chamber, or a vast network of connecting chambers. Groundwater filled with dissolved minerals drips, slips, and puddles inside caves. The minerals crystallize and create the icicle-like stone formations called stalactites and stalagmites. One way to remember which is which is that stalactites (with a *c*) *cling* to the *ceiling,* while stalagmites (with a *g*) *grow* from the *ground.* Sometimes a stalactite grows so long that it connects with a stalagmite. Together, they form a column.

SUGGESTIONS FOR FURTHER READING

Branley, Franklyn M. *Volcanoes*. Illustrated by Megan Lloyd. New York: HarperCollins, 2008.

Hooper, Meredith. *The Drop in My Drink: The Story of Water on Our Planet*. Illustrated by Chris Coady. New York: Viking, 1998.

Patent, Dorothy Hinshaw. *Shaping the Earth*. Photographs by William Muñoz. New York: Clarion, 2000.

Prager, Ellen J. *Earthquakes*. Illustrated by Susan Greenman. Washington, DC: National Geographic, 2002.

Rusch, Elizabeth. *Eruption! Volcanoes and the Science of Saving Lives*. Photographs by Tom Uhlman. Boston: Houghton Mifflin Harcourt, 2013.

Simon, Seymour. *Oceans*. Washington, DC: Smithsonian, 2006.

Strauss, Rochelle. *One Well: The Story of Water on Earth*. Illustrated by Rosemary Woods. Toronto, ON: Kids Can Press, 2007.

Walker, Sally M. *Figuring Out Fossils*. Minneapolis: Lerner, 2013.

———. *Glaciers*. Minneapolis: Lerner, 2008.

———. *Marveling at Minerals*. Minneapolis: Lerner, 2013.

———. *Researching Rocks*. Minneapolis: Lerner, 2013.

Wells, Robert E. *Did a Dinosaur Drink This Water?* Morton Grove, IL: Albert Whitman, 2006.